All About

100+ Amazing & Interesting Facts

that everyone should know

that everyone should know

Introduction

Filled with up-to-date information, fascinating & fun facts this book " All About France: 100+ Amazing & Interesting Facts that everyone should know" is the best book for kids to find out more about the largest country in the European Union. This book would satisfy the children's curiosity and help them to understand why France is a bucket-list trip for many—and what makes it different from other European nations. This book gives a story, history & explores the country's best cuisine, architecture, fashion, art, language, people, places and many more. It is a fun and fascinating way for young readers to find out more interesting facts. This is a great chance for every kid to expand their knowledge about France and impress family and friends with all "discovered and never knew before" amazing facts.

1. France is the largest country in the European Union and the third-largest country in Europe, behind Ukraine and the European portion of Russia.

2. France also sometimes referred to as 'the hexagon' due to its six-sided shape.

3. France shares land borders with eight countries. The bordering countries of France are Belgium, Germany, Luxembourg, Switzerland, Italy, Monaco, Andorra, and Spain. The longest border is shared with Spain and the shortest with Monaco.

4. After Germany, France has the second-largest population of EU nations and 85% of its population lives in urban areas.

5. Before being named France, the land was called Gaul (Latin: Gallia; French: Gaule).

6. The actual name "France" came from a Germanic tribe. They used the word "frank", which meant "free" in their native language.

7. Paris is the capital and the most populous city of France.

8. Paris is known as 'The City of Love', 'Fashion Capital of the World', and 'Literary Paradise'.

9. Paris was one of the first cities in the world to install streetlights.
10. Paris was ranked as the second most visited travel destination in the world in 2019, after Bangkok and just ahead of London.

11. After Singapore, Paris is the second most expensive city in the world.

12. Many people from all over the world come to Paris for shopping because it is famous in the world for its fashion and culture.

13. Despite the incredible amount of traffic, there is only one "Stop" sign in the entire city of Paris. There are "No Left Turn" signs as well as "Do Not Enter" signs, but only one red octagonal "Stop" sign.

14. The Eiffel Tower is named after its engineer, 'Alexandre-Gustave Eiffel.' It is one of the most recognized structures in the world.

15. It is painted every seven years, taking five tons of paint to complete the job each time.

16. The Eiffel Tower is the most-visited paid monument in the world. It was built in 1889.

17. The Eiffel Tower was the tallest man-made structure in the world for almost 41 years until the erection of the Chrysler Building in New York City in 1930.

18. The Statue of Liberty was a gift from the people of France to the

United States of America. It was built by Alexandre-Gustave Eiffel, the man who also constructed the Eiffel Tower.

19. There are currently ten Statues of Liberty in France, with five in Paris alone.

20. Even though the population of France is approximately 66 million, it is a geographically large country. This results in an exceptionally low population density of about 295 people per square mile.

21. The official motto of the French Republic is "Liberty, Equality, Fraternity".

22. The national flag is "The Flag of France".

23. The Flag of France is a tricolor, and consists in three vertical stripes of equal width, colored in royal blue, white, and red.

24. "La Marseillaise" is the national anthem of France. The song was written in 1792 by Claude Joseph Rouget de Lisle.

25. The Great Seal of France is the official seal of the French Republic.

26. The Great Seal Features Liberty personified as a seated Juno wearing a crown with seven arches. 27. She holds fasces and is supported by a ship's tiller with a cock printed on it. At her feet is a vase with the letters "SU" At her right, in the background, are symbols of the arts (painter's tools), architecture (Ionic order), education (burning lamp), agriculture (a sheaf of wheat) and industry (a cog wheel). The scene

is surrounded by the legend French Republic, democratic, one and indivisible and 24 February 1848 at the bottom.

28. The current coat of arms of France has been a symbol of France since 1953.

29. French, the official language, is the first language of 88% of the population.

30. Catholicism is the largest religion in France.

31. Bastille Day is the national day of France, which is celebrated on 14 July each year.

32. The French National Convention adopted it as the Republic's anthem in 1795.

33. The national currency of France is Euro.

34. The French franc was the currency of France until the euro was adopted in 1999.

35. France is one of the most sports-oriented countries in the world. It hosts many prestigious international tournaments every year and France is one of the leading winners of gold medals in Olympics.

36. The national game of France is Football. It is the most popular sports in France.

37. The Tour de France is the world's most famous cycling event and finishes on the historical stretch of the Champs-Élysée in Paris.

38. The national tree of France is Taxus baccata. It is the native tree of south and western Europe. It is also known as Yew or European Yew.

39. The national flower of France is Iris flower. The meaning of the iris is Rainbow. There are many colors of iris, including blue, pink, purple, white, and yellow. It has almost 200 species.

40. The national animal of France is Gallic Rooster.

41. The national drink of France is Pastis.

42. French national forest is the national forest of France.

43. The Loire is the longest river of France with about 1,006 km.

44. The national dish of France is pot-au-feu. This is a type of dish

which provides both as boiled meat and vegetables and a soup.

45. France produces over 400 varieties of cheese.

46. French fries and French toast are NOT French inventions.

47. The national dessert of France is Clafoutis. It is a baked French dessert of fruits, culturally topped with black cherries.

48. The national river of France is The Seine river. The length of this river is 777 km. It is the main source of water in the Paris Basin in the north of France.

49. The national mountain of France is Mont blanc. The meaning of the Mont Blanc is ''White

Mountain''. It is the highest mountain in the Alps.

50. The largest lake in France is the spectacular Lake Geneva. It covers 582 square kilometers.
51. The Pyrenées are the longest mountain range in France.
52. The highest mountain in France is the Mont Blanc, that is 15,780 ft high and stands at the border between France and Italy. This is

the second highest mountain in Europe after Mount Elbrus.

53. The national museum of France is the National Museum of Natural History. In French, it is known as the Museum national d'histoire Naturelle.

54. The national poet of France are Victor Hugo and Charles Baudelaire.

55. France has more Nobel Prize winners in Literature than any other country. They are also one of the top countries to have awards in Physiology, Medicine, and Physics.

56. The national color of France is red, white, and blue.

57. The national library of France is BnF. It is situated in Paris. The origin of this library is the Royal

Library at Louvre Palace made by Charles V in 1368.

58. At a total length of 29,000km, the French railway network is the second biggest in Europe and the ninth biggest in the world.
59. The national stadium of France is Stade De France. It is situated in Saint-Denis in the north of Paris.

60. France uses nuclear power for 79% of its electricity, making it the largest user of nuclear power in the world.

61. 99% of 15 and older population of France are literate.

62. The national airline of France is Air France. It is the secondary of Air France-KLM. It is the founding member of Sky Team global airline.

63. French is the second most studied language in the world, right behind English.

64. Grasse in France is known as the World's Capital of Perfume.

65. France is the first country to make throwing out or burning food illegal.

66. The University of Paris or the "La Sorbonne" Europe's oldest university is in France.

67. There are 12 time zones in use in France. This is the highest number among any nation in the world.

68. The parachute, the hot air balloon, the motion picture camera, the bicycle, and inflatable tires for cars are all French inventions.

69. Marie Curie, Blaise Pascal, Pierre Curie, Louis Pasteur and

Joseph Fourier are some of the famous scientists from France.

70. All roads in the country have a point where they all start. This point is named Point Zero, and it is marked by a bronze star that is set on the pavement near the Notre Dame Cathedral's main entrance in Paris.

71. The French sleep the most among people in the developed world. On average, they sleep 8.83 hours per day.

72. Paris has many of the world's most famous art pieces including the Mona Lisa and Venus de Milo. These works of art can be seen in the Louvre Museum, which is among the world's largest museums.

73. Due to France's moderate climate and an abundant amount of usable farmland, they are the European leader in agriculture.

74. France is the world's second-largest exporter of agricultural products.

75. Europe's busiest railway station and one of the oldest in the world is Paris Gare du Nord. 190 million passengers go through the station each year.

76. The world's first true department store was opened in Paris in 1838.

77. Louis XIX was the king of France for just 20 minutes, the shortest ever reign.

78. There Are Over 500 Islands in France.

79. In 2017, French President Emmanuel Macron became the youngest ever President of his country at the age of 39.

80. France was the 1st country to ban throwing away of excess food.

81 Turning a baguette upside down is unlucky in France.

82 It is estimated that 94% of French children know English as their second language.

83. French is the official language of 24 countries in the world.

84. French was the official language of England for about 300 years, from 1066 to 1362.

85. French life expectancy for men is 78, while the average for women is 84. When compared to the rest of

the world, this indicates that the French are very healthy.

86. Parents who successfully raise several children with dignity are awarded the Medal of the French Family (La Médaille de La Famille Française) by the government.

87. Potatoes were once illegal in France. Between 1748 and 1772 French thought that potatoes caused leprosy.

88. France was one of the first countries to broadcast regular television programming. TV came to France in 1931.

89. The oldest person who ever lived was a French woman named Jeanne Louise Calment.

90. Jeanne Louise Calment has lived122 years and 164 days. She was born in France on 21 February 1875 and died on 4 August 1997.

91. The tradition of wearing a white dress for wedding days originated in France back in 1499.

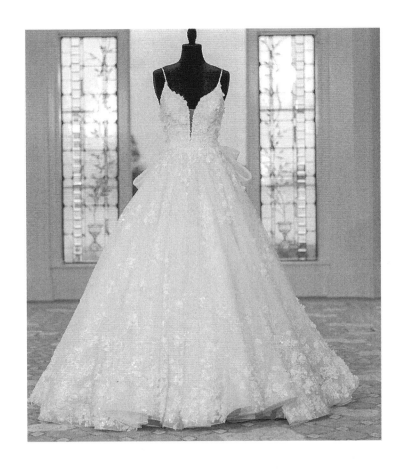

91. Paris holds an annual competition for the best baguette. Whoever wins would get the ultimate opportunity to bake for the president of France for a year.

92.

93. In France, it is illegal to name a pig "Napoleon."

94. More people in Africa speak French than people in France.

95. The word "entrepreneur" was also invented by the French.

95. The Notre Dame is the most visited monument/attraction in France. The cathedral Notre Dame receives more than 14 million visitors per year.

96. France has 37 sites inscribed in UNESCO's World Heritage List and features cities of high cultural interest, beaches and seaside resorts, ski resorts, and rural regions that many enjoy for their beauty and tranquility.

97. France was the first nation to introduce the concept of license plates for automobiles in 1893.

98. In France, it is illegal to take images of police officers or their vehicles, even in the background.

99. The French president Charles de Gaulle has survived 32 assassination attempts, the most in the world by anyone.

100. With more than 10 million tourists a year, the French Riviera (or Côte d'Azur), in south-east France, is the second leading tourist destination in the country.

101. The Louvre Museum in Paris is consistently the most visited museum in the world. Over 9

million visitors go through their doors annually.

102. Disneyland Paris, despite the name, is not located in Paris itself, but can be found about 30 km away from Paris in a place called Marne-la-Vallée. More than 15 million people visit this place each year.

Please check this out:
Our other best-selling books for kids are-
Know about Sharks: 100 Amazing Fun Facts with Pictures
Know About Whales:100+ Amazing & Interesting Fun Facts with Pictures: " Never known Before "- Whale's facts
Know About Dinosaurs: 100 Amazing & Interesting Fun Facts with Pictures
Know About Kangaroos: Amazing & Interesting Facts with Pictures
Know About Penguins: 100+ Amazing Penguin Facts with Pictures
Know About Dolphins :100 Amazing Dolphin Facts with Pictures
Know About Elephant
All About New York: 100+ Amazing Facts with Pictures
All About New Jersey: 100+ Amazing Facts with Pictures

All About Massachusetts: 100+
Amazing Facts with Pictures
All About Florida: 100+ Amazing Facts
with Pictures
All About California: 100+ Amazing
Facts with Pictures
All About Arizona: 100+ Amazing Facts
with Pictures
All About Texas: 100+ Amazing Facts
with Pictures
All About Minnesota: 100+ Amazing
Facts with Pictures
All About Italy: 100+ Amazing Facts
with Pictures
100 Amazing Quiz Q & A About
Penguin: Never Known Before Penguin
Facts
Most Popular Animal Quiz book for
Kids: 100 amazing animal facts
Quiz Book for Kids: Science, History,
Geography, Biology, Computer &
Information Technology

English Grammar for Kids: Most Easy Way to learn English Grammar

Solar System & Space Science- Quiz for Kids: What You Know About Solar System

English Grammar Practice Book for elementary kids: 1000+ Practice Questions with Answers

A to Z of English Tense

My First Fruits

Printed in Great Britain
by Amazon

66095091R00025